To my friend Leila, for her infinite
joy in life's minute details.

First paperback edition published in 2023 by Flying Eye Books.

First published in 2018 by Flying Eye Books Ltd. 27 Westgate Street, London, E8 3RL.

Text and illustrations © Owen Davey 2018.

Owen Davey has asserted his right under the Copyright, Designs and Patents Act,
1988, to be identified as the Author and Illustrator of this Work.

Scientific consultant: Dr Rosalyn Wade

Every attempt has been made to ensure any statements written as fact have been checked
to the best of our abilities. However, we are still human, thankfully, and occasionally
little mistakes may crop up. Should you spot any errors, please email info@nobrow.net.

1 3 5 7 9 10 8 6 4 2

Published in the US by Flying Eye Books Ltd.
Printed in Poland on FSC® certified paper

ISBN: 978-1-83874-872-2
www.flyingeyebooks.com

OWEN DAVEY

BONKERS ABOUT BEETLES

FLYING EYE BOOKS

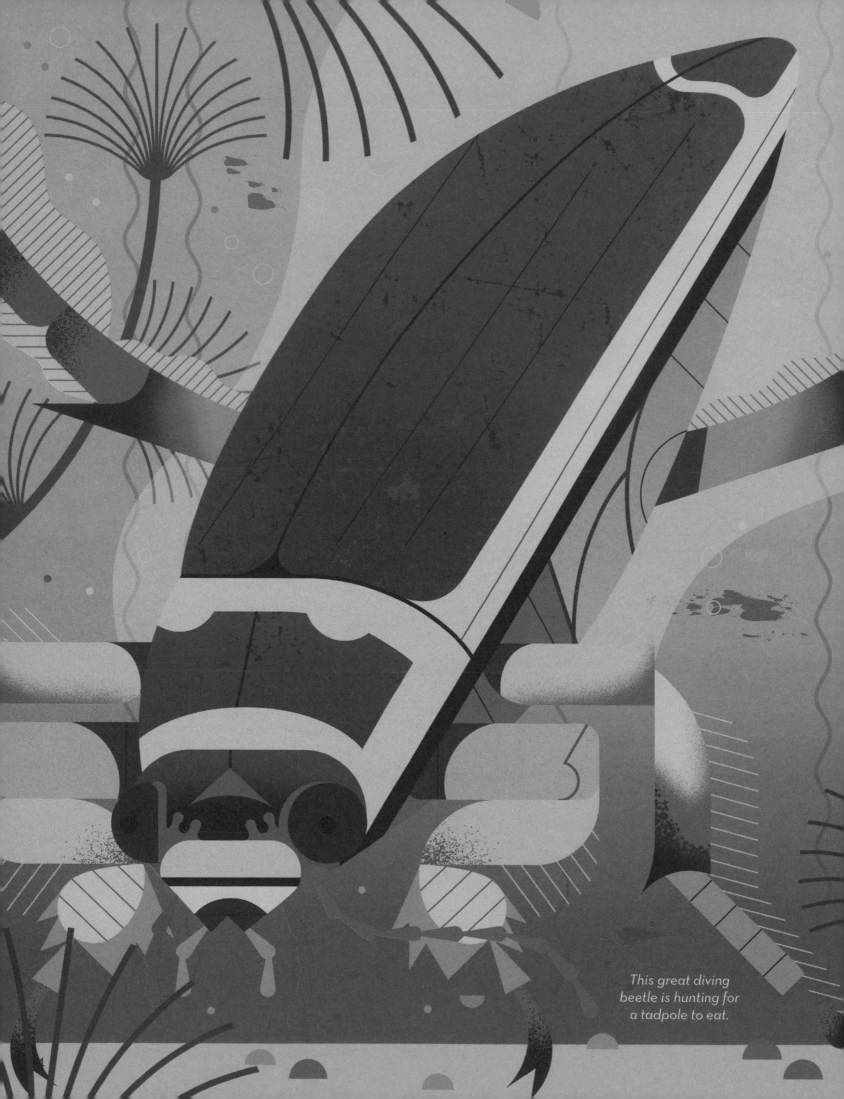

This great diving beetle is hunting for a tadpole to eat.

CONTENTS

WHAT ARE BEETLES?

Beetles are a group of insects. They have six legs, three body segments, and two feelers sticking out of their heads. Beetles are different from most other insects in that their forewings form a hard or leathery protective case over their backs. Somebody who studies beetles is known as a "coleopterist." Due to the vast number of beetle types, not all of them have been given common (and easy to pronounce) names, so coleopterists use the Latin terms for them instead.

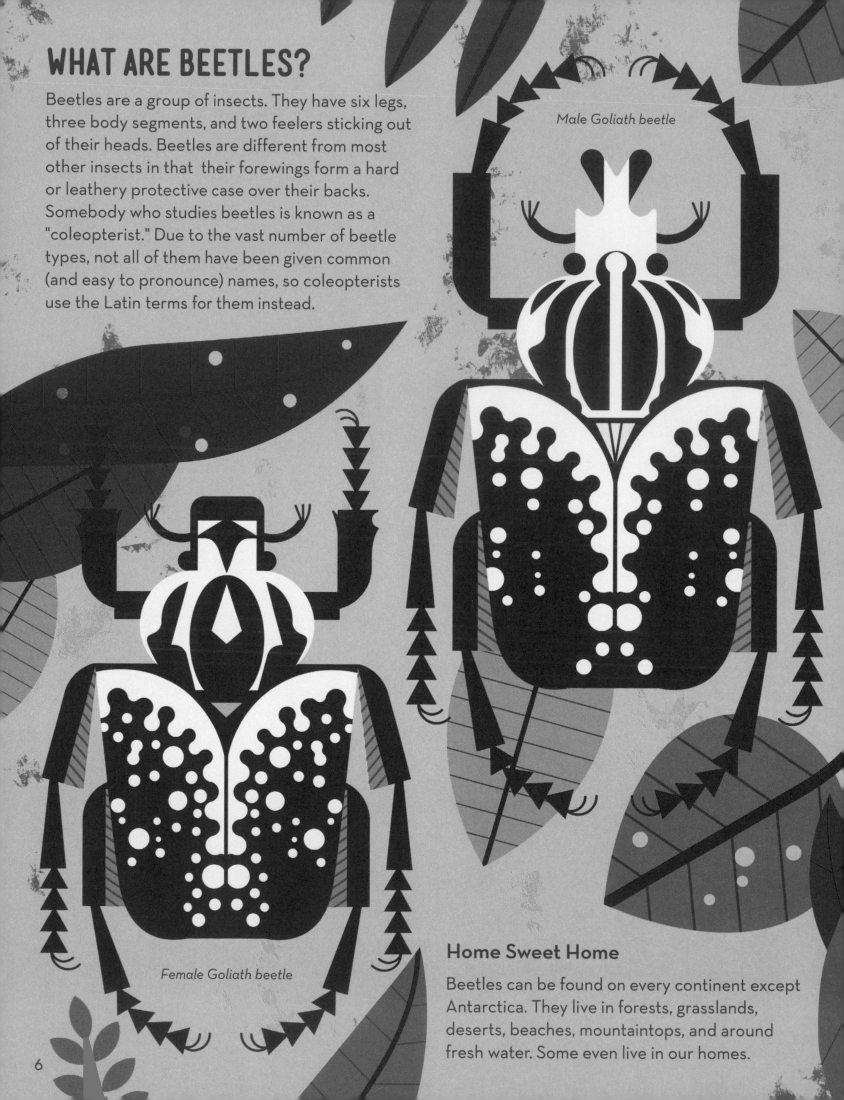

Male Goliath beetle

Female Goliath beetle

Home Sweet Home

Beetles can be found on every continent except Antarctica. They live in forests, grasslands, deserts, beaches, mountaintops, and around fresh water. Some even live in our homes.

Nom Nom

Together, different beetle species eat every part of a plant, from the leaves right down to the roots. Some prefer to hunt other creatures or feed on the remains of dead animals. Beetles may eat pollen, pinecones, worms, wool, other insects including caterpillars and beetles, frogs, fruit, cereal, dog biscuits, and even poop. Yep, you read that right... poop!

The varied diet of beetles.

So now that you know the basics, let's pick up our magnifying glasses and delve into the wonders of the undergrowth. Are you ready to go *Bonkers About Beetles*?

A WAY OF LIFE

Beetles account for a quarter of all the discovered animal species in the world. Biologists have found around 400,000 different beetle species living on our planet, but some believe there may be more than 2 million. With so many beetles around, it's not surprising that they've adapted to all kinds of lifestyles, habitats, and diets. Here's a guide to their ways of life.

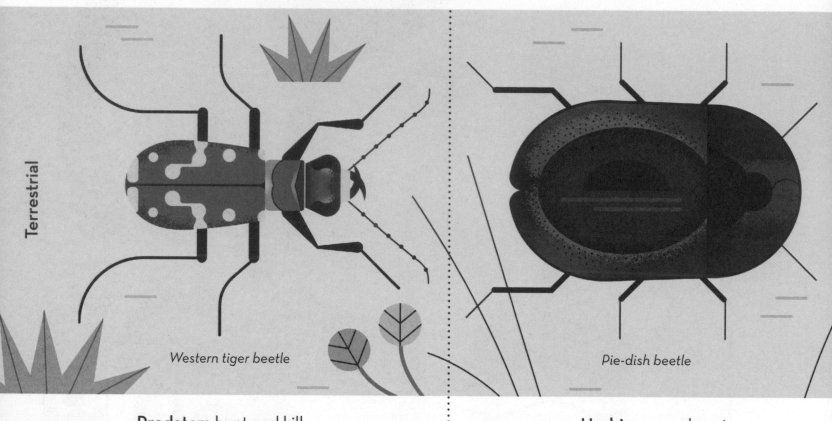

Terrestrial

Western tiger beetle

Pie-dish beetle

Predators hunt and kill other animals for food.

Herbivores only eat plant-based food.

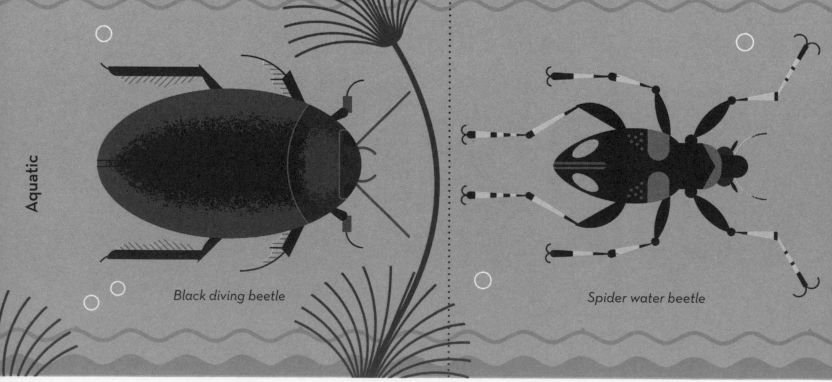

Aquatic

Black diving beetle

Spider water beetle

Terrestrial animals live on dry land.

Aquatic animals live in water. Most aquatic beetle species live in fresh water, but some live in the sea, close to the shore.

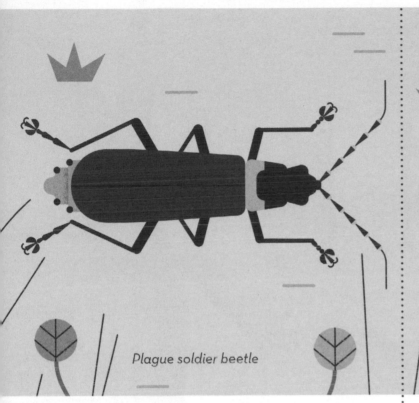

Plague soldier beetle

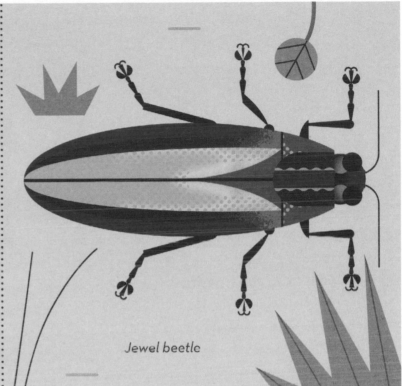

Jewel beetle

Omnivores feed on both animals and plants.

Decomposers break down and eat dead and decaying animals or plants.

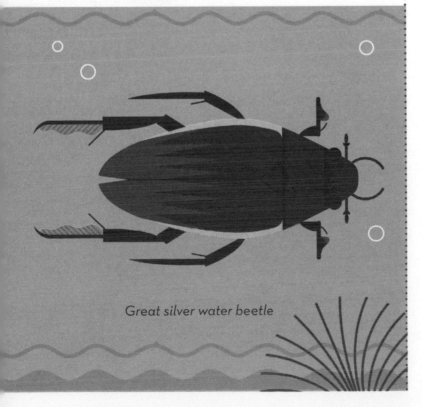

Great silver water beetle

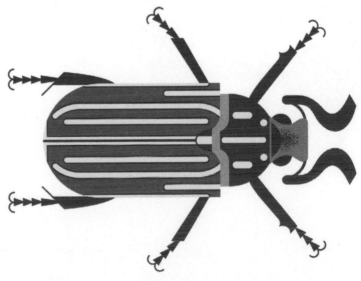

The ten-lined June beetle feeds on leaves and pine needles. Can you figure out where on the chart it would fit?

BY DESIGN

Beetles come in a wide range of shapes and sizes, but all have a similar design. Take a closer look at this Japanese beetle to discover the secrets of their survival.

1. Pronotum

An armored plate that sits on the front part of a beetle's thorax. Sometimes this area has horns on it, which are usually used for fighting.

2. Antennae

For sensing smell, vibrations, and temperature. Antennae can look very different from one beetle to the next.

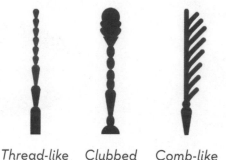

Thread-like *Clubbed* *Comb-like*

3. Elytra

Hard forewings that protect the delicate flight wings. When taking off, the elytra swing out of the way and can help stabilize a beetle's flight. Some beetles can even capture air bubbles under their elytra to help them breathe underwater.

Japanese rhinoceros beetle

4. Horns

Some males have extraordinary horns on their heads, which can be used to headbutt, block, pry, or lift rival males away from females.

5. Legs

For climbing, crawling, running, jumping, burrowing, or swimming.

Spiracles

Beetles don't have lungs. Instead, air passes through little openings in their bodies called spiracles.

Exoskeleton

Unlike humans, beetles have very hard skeletons on the outside of their bodies.

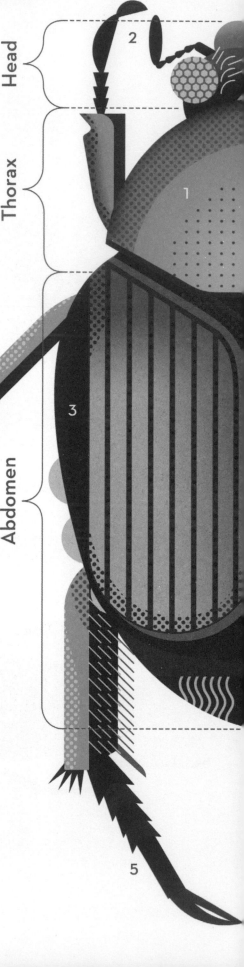

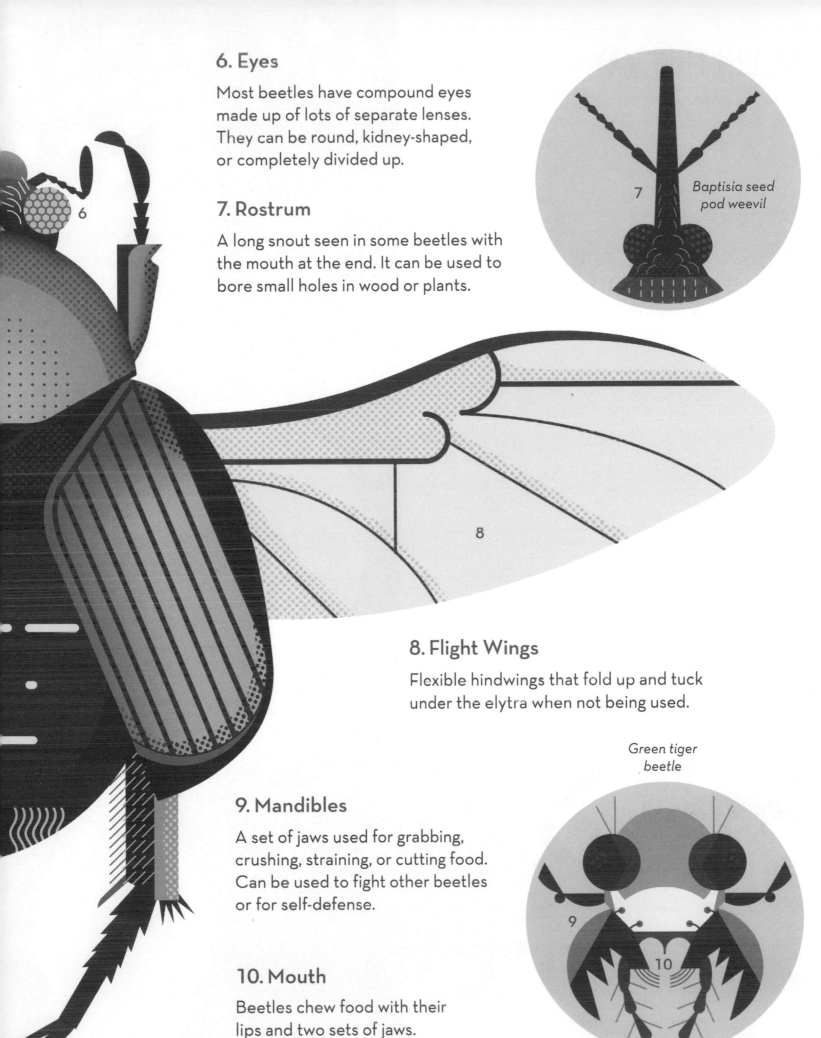

6. Eyes

Most beetles have compound eyes made up of lots of separate lenses. They can be round, kidney-shaped, or completely divided up.

7. Rostrum

A long snout seen in some beetles with the mouth at the end. It can be used to bore small holes in wood or plants.

7 *Baptisia seed pod weevil*

8. Flight Wings

Flexible hindwings that fold up and tuck under the elytra when not being used.

Green tiger beetle

9. Mandibles

A set of jaws used for grabbing, crushing, straining, or cutting food. Can be used to fight other beetles or for self-defense.

10. Mouth

Beetles chew food with their lips and two sets of jaws.

BORN THIS WAY

Beetles undergo several complete changes as they grow up. At each stage in its life cycle, a beetle will look and behave very differently. The changes from egg to adult are called a "metamorphosis" and can take anywhere from a few months up to 50 years.

Egg

Beetles start their lives as eggs. Parent stag beetles bury their eggs in soil or near a good food source for their young.

Larva

When the egg hatches, a larva appears. The job of the larva is to eat and grow.

As the larva gets bigger, it grows new skin, shedding the old skin in the process. Each of these larval stages is known as an "instar."

Pupa

When the larva is ready, it will "pupate." It builds a casing around itself and transforms into a soft version of its adult form. Eventually, the exoskeleton hardens and the beetle emerges as an adult.

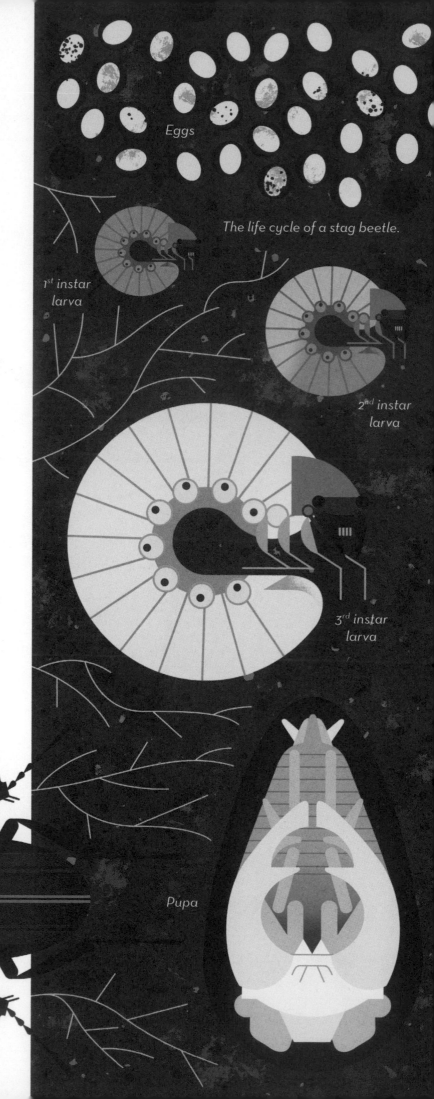

Eggs

The life cycle of a stag beetle.

1st instar larva

2nd instar larva

3rd instar larva

Pupa

Adult stag beetle

Love You and Leaf You

Leaf-rolling weevils use their legs and jaws to cut and fold leaves into nests for their eggs. *Pilolabus viridans* beetles take about two hours to construct the uniquely rounded home for their eggs. When they hatch, the larvae develop inside the leaf ball.

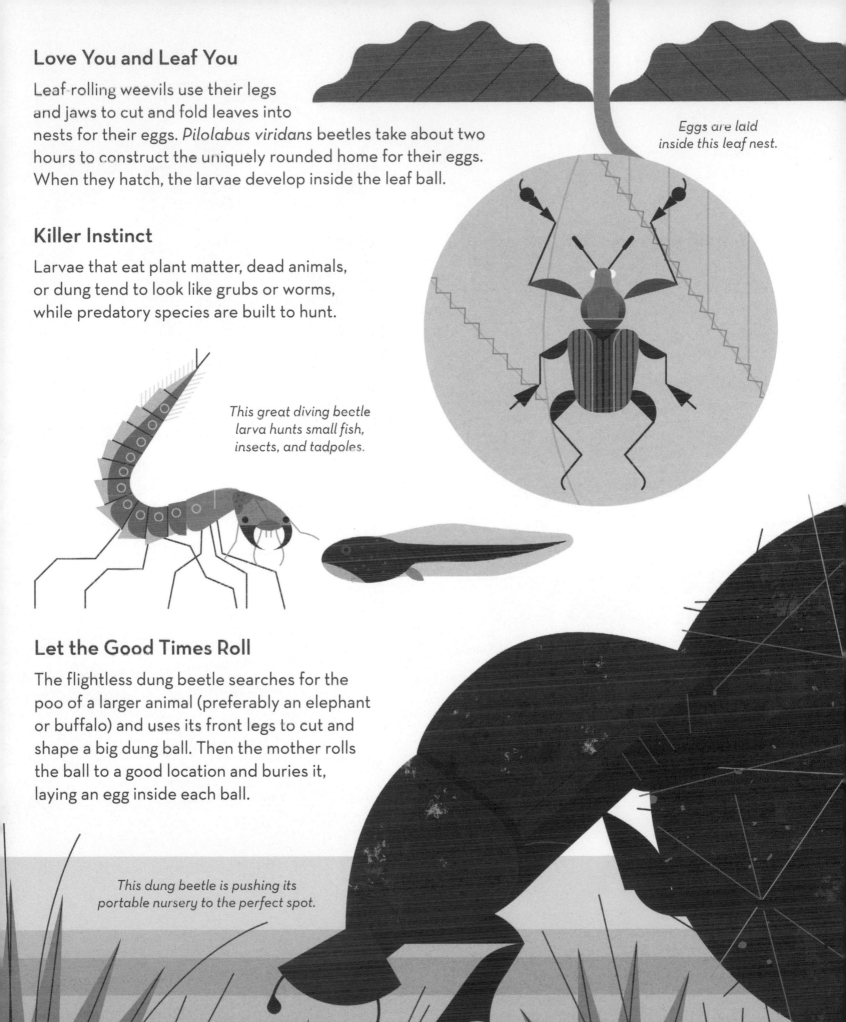

Eggs are laid inside this leaf nest.

Killer Instinct

Larvae that eat plant matter, dead animals, or dung tend to look like grubs or worms, while predatory species are built to hunt.

This great diving beetle larva hunts small fish, insects, and tadpoles.

Let the Good Times Roll

The flightless dung beetle searches for the poo of a larger animal (preferably an elephant or buffalo) and uses its front legs to cut and shape a big dung ball. Then the mother rolls the ball to a good location and buries it, laying an egg inside each ball.

This dung beetle is pushing its portable nursery to the perfect spot.

COME TO LIGHT

Featured Creatures: Fireflies

The *Lampyridae* family are more commonly known as fireflies, lightning bugs, or glow-worms. These beetles use chemicals in their bodies to create beautiful light shows with their abdomens. This is called "bioluminescence." Fireflies usually use their light flashes to find each other in the dark, or to warn predators that they are poisonous to eat.

Male fireflies glow to impress. If any females like what they see, they flash back to help the male find them. It's very much like a glowing version of the game Marco Polo.

Lightning-bug firefly

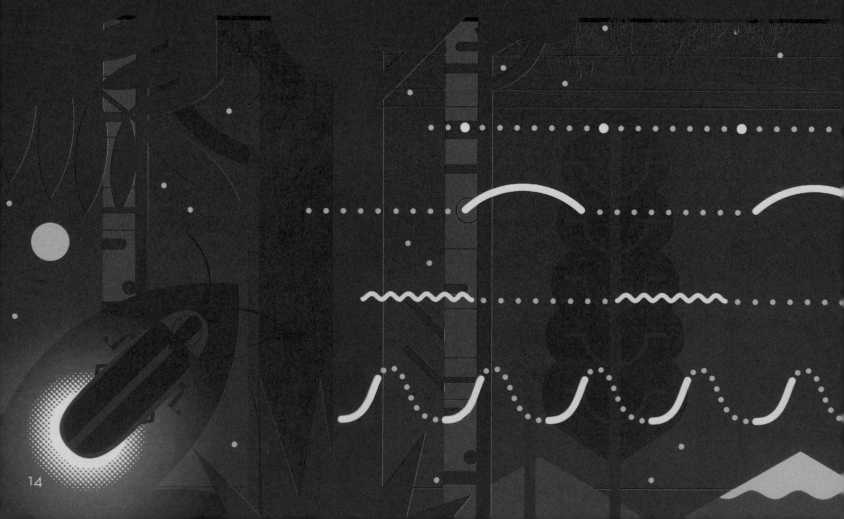

*Common
eastern firefly*

Some fireflies can synchronise their flash patterns, creating a choreographed light show by glowing on and off at the same time. Some studies suggest that the females are more responsive to synchronised males.

Pennsylvania firefly females mimic the light signals of other fireflies to lure in romancing males of other species. Any poor firefly tricked by this cunning ploy is eaten alive. The males use this mimicry to their advantage, pretending to be prey species in order to entice females to them for mating.

The flight path

The flash pattern

*Photinus ignitus fly straight,
flashing every 5.1 seconds.*

*Photinus collustrans create an arc in
the air while flashing for 0.4 seconds.*

*Photinus granulatus zig-zag
and flash every other second.*

*The common eastern firefly has a distinctive
long flash shaped like the letter J.*

MAKING A MEAL OF THINGS

While some carnivorous beetles simply chase their prey down, many others go to great lengths or use clever tactics to find their next meal.

These sneaky beetle larvae find a smart way to infiltrate the bees' stronghold.

A North American beaver and a beaver beetle.

Beaver beetles are very flat and have no eyes or wings, but they thrive by feeding on the skin of beavers. They live as parasites, which means that the beavers do not benefit from these tiny hitchhikers.

Black oil beetles lay their eggs in burrows near flowers. The larvae climb onto the flower and attach themselves to visiting bees. They are carried back to the nest, where they feed on the bees' eggs.

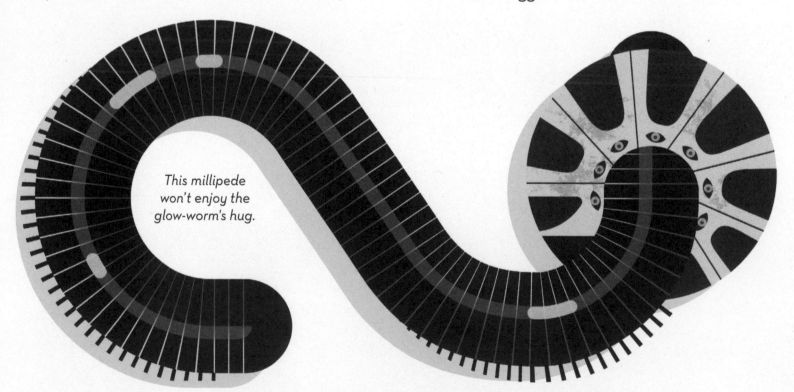

This millipede won't enjoy the glow-worm's hug.

The larva of the Western banded glow-worm chases after millipedes, coiling its body around the millipede's head and biting it. Once the millipede stops moving, the glow-worm forces its way inside and starts to feed.

Head-stander beetles live in the dry Namib desert in southern Africa, where it can be difficult to find a drink. These beetles strategically climb to the top of sand dunes early in the morning when there's a water-filled fog in the air. They lift their bottoms to the sky so that the water collects on their backs and runs down into their mouths.

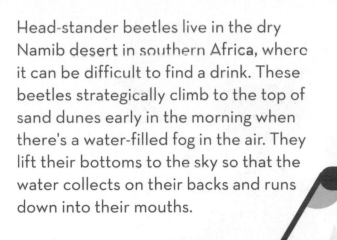

Bottoms up! A well-earned drink of water.

An Epomis dejeani larva eating a frog.

This ground beetle larva feeds only on amphibians, including frogs and salamanders. It lures its prey by wiggling its antennae and jaws to look as delicious as possible. When the amphibian strikes, the larva dodges the attack and sinks its jaws into the unsuspecting creature.

DRESS FOR SUCCESS

Beetles can be a stunning array of colors, patterns, and shapes. It's not all for show, however, as these characteristics can be key to their survival. They help them to avoid the deathly gaze of predators or stay hidden from their prey.

The appearance of many beetles acts as a warning code for predators. Known as "aposematism," distinctive color patterns display to the world that these beetles would not make a good meal. The beetles may be poisonous, well-defended, or sometimes just taste really bad.

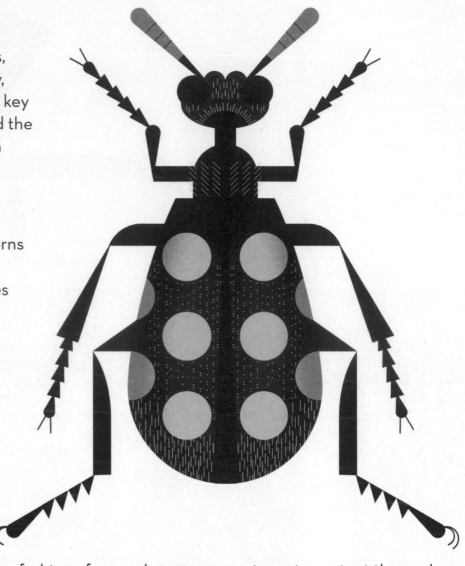

The yellow and black pattern of this Hycleus lugens warns that its body contains burning liquid.

Some harmless species of beetle copy the fashion of more dangerous creatures to protect themselves. These beetles copy the shape, color, and even the behavior of species that are known to bite, sting, or chemically defend themselves. A possible predator may think twice before trying it for dinner!

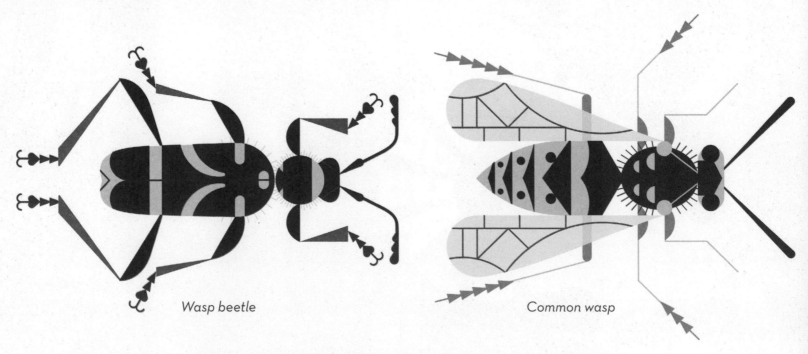

Wasp beetle

Common wasp

This wasp beetle has copied the colors of a wasp, an insect well known for its powerful sting. It also buzzes like a wasp when threatened.

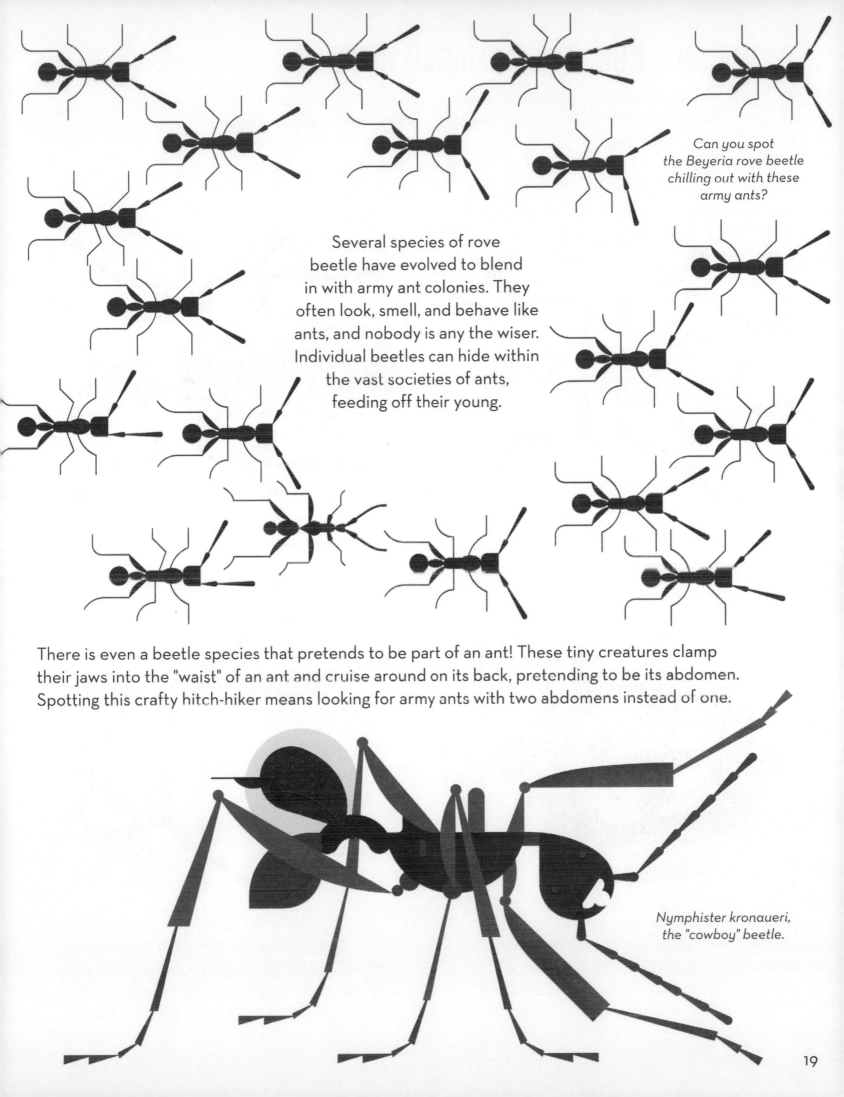

Can you spot the Beyeria rove beetle chilling out with these army ants?

Several species of rove beetle have evolved to blend in with army ant colonies. They often look, smell, and behave like ants, and nobody is any the wiser. Individual beetles can hide within the vast societies of ants, feeding off their young.

There is even a beetle species that pretends to be part of an ant! These tiny creatures clamp their jaws into the "waist" of an ant and cruise around on its back, pretending to be its abdomen. Spotting this crafty hitch-hiker means looking for army ants with two abdomens instead of one.

Nymphister kronaueri, the "cowboy" beetle.

YOU CAN'T RUN, BUT YOU CAN HIDE

How about hiding in plain sight? "Camouflage" is when something blends in with its surroundings, making it hard to see. Many beetles use camouflage, from being a similar color to their habitat, to mimicking the pattern of poo. Some weevils have taken their disguises even further by growing miniature gardens on their backs. When standing still, they look like nothing more than a pile of moss.

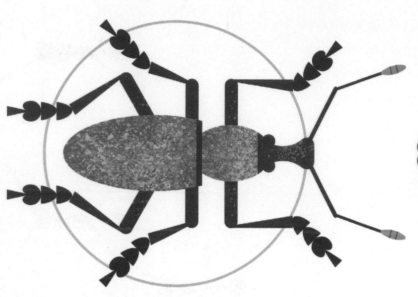

This *Gymnopholus wichmanni* is covered in lichen and algae.

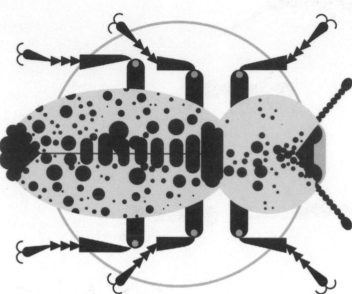

The flecked pattern on the heavily-armored Texas ironclad beetle makes it look like bird poo.

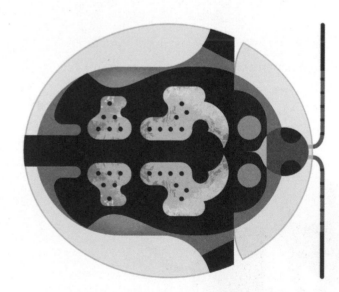

The mottled tortoise beetle has a hard exoskeleton that covers its head and body. When threatened, it pulls its legs and antennae under this umbrella-like structure and attaches itself to a leaf.

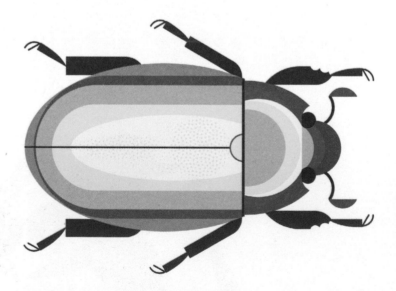

The exoskeleton of this species of scarab beetle reflects the sun so magnificently that it looks like polished gold. You might think this would make it an easy target in a dark forest habitat, but the shine seems to confuse predators.

Can you spot the impressive longhorn beetle against this tree?

A FORM OF SELF-DEFENSE

Beetles have a number of elaborate defenses to protect them from danger and ensure their survival.

Drop Dead

What do you do if you're out in the open, munching away on your favorite leaf, and something attacks you? According to many weevil species, the answer is simple: you fall over. By letting themselves drop to the ground, gravity provides them with a rapid getaway. Some species also stay completely still, playing dead while predators investigate their bodies. The would-be attacker is looking for living prey, so it quickly loses interest in a seemingly dead meal.

Polydrusus formosus

Boom! Boom! Boom!

How about a bit of firepower? The bombardier beetle combines chemicals in its body and takes aim. With a loud popping sound, it releases an explosion of burning liquid from its rear, squirting it directly at attackers.

Pheropsophus verticalis

Secret Weapon

This species of longhorn beetle found in Brazil has a unique ability among insects. Its antennae look like scorpion's tails and can deliver poisonous stings to keep predators at bay.

Onychocerus albitarsis

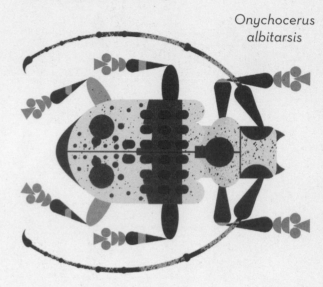

That Stinks

When alarmed, stink beetles release a terrible smell into the air. People have described this putrid stench as something close to the smell of moldy cheese or a dead rat.

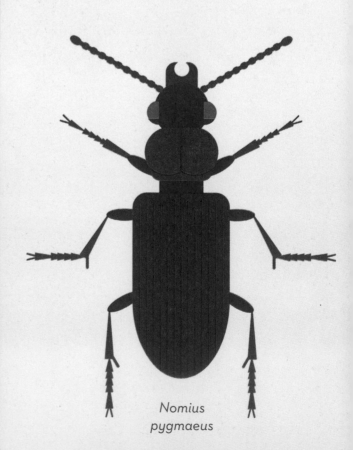

Nomius pygmaeus

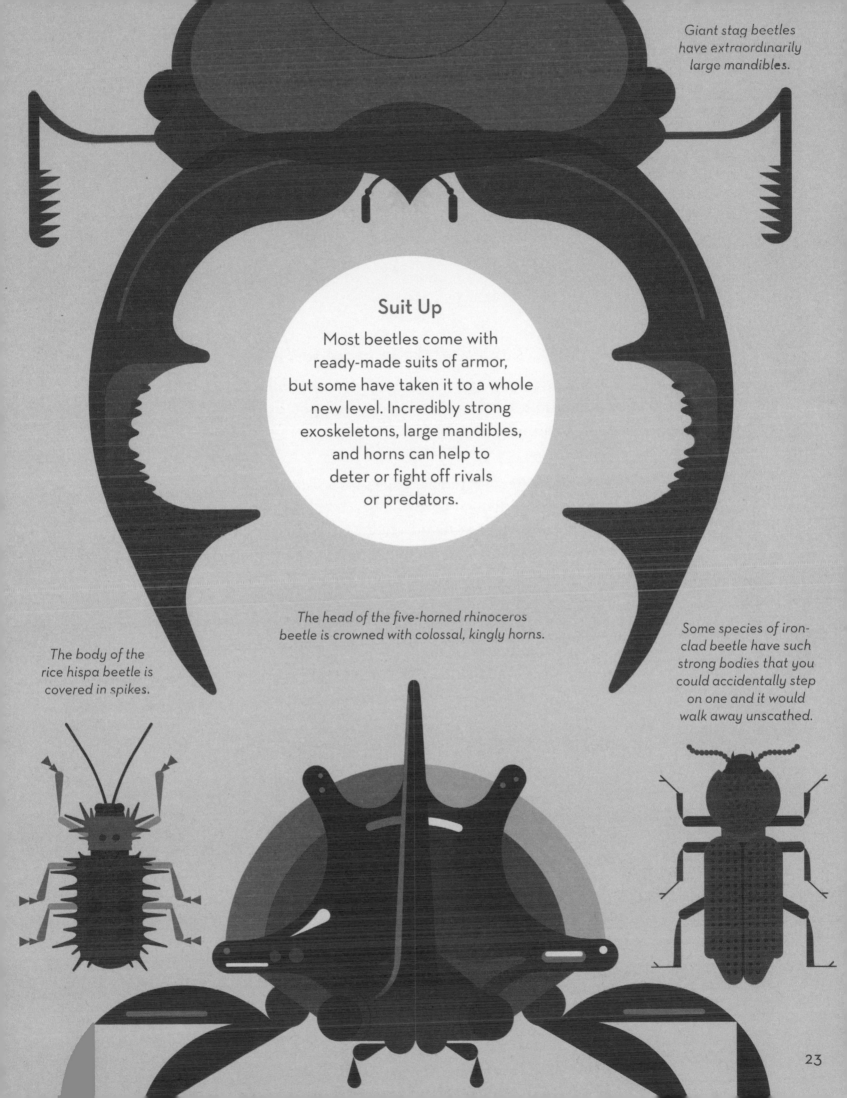

Giant stag beetles have extraordinarily large mandibles.

Suit Up

Most beetles come with ready-made suits of armor, but some have taken it to a whole new level. Incredibly strong exoskeletons, large mandibles, and horns can help to deter or fight off rivals or predators.

The head of the five-horned rhinoceros beetle is crowned with colossal, kingly horns.

The body of the rice hispa beetle is covered in spikes.

Some species of iron-clad beetle have such strong bodies that you could accidentally step on one and it would walk away unscathed.

Featured Creatures: Seven-spot Ladybug

Seven-spot ladybugs are probably the most famous of all beetle species. They are easy to "spot" by their iconic pattern of seven black blotches on bright red (sometimes orange or yellow) elytra.

In winter, when the temperature falls and less food is available, ladybugs need to hibernate. Hibernation is when an animal goes into a deep sleep to save energy. During hibernation, ladybugs may seek shelter in dead leaves, hollow stems of plants, or even under tree bark. Many individuals can sometimes be seen huddling together in the same location.

The popularity of ladybugs is mainly due to the unpopularity of their prey: the aphid. Aphids are small sap-eating insects that can devastate crops and gardens, but ladybugs are thought to be able to consume around 5,000 aphids in a single year!

The warning colors of red and black tell predators such as birds that these critters are toxic, but ladybugs have a secret weapon just in case. Adults ooze yucky-tasting liquid from the joints in their legs. Meal ruined.

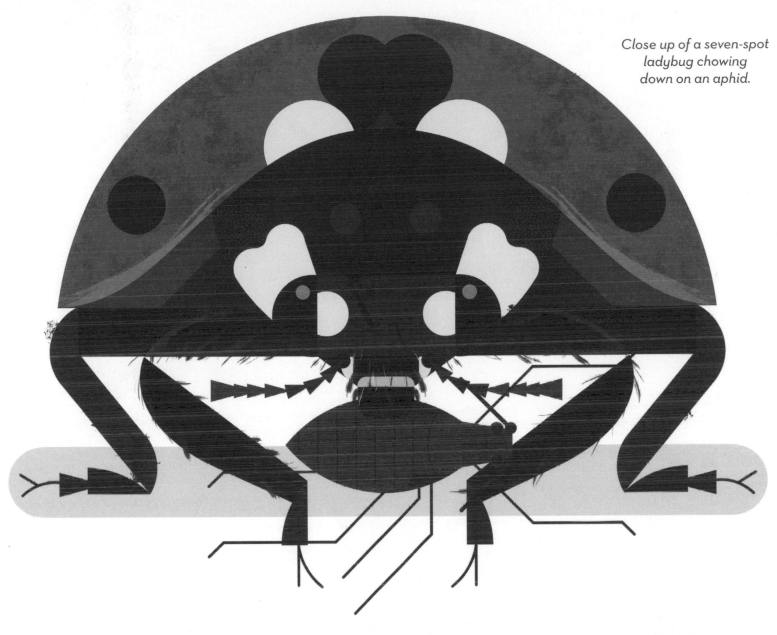

Close up of a seven-spot ladybug chowing down on an aphid.

There are over 6,000 described species of ladybugs around the world. Here are a just a few species:

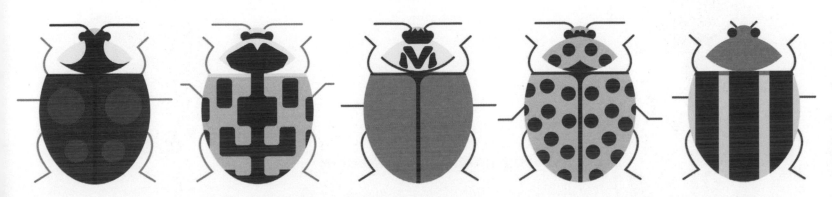

Harlequin ladybugs have been described with over 100 color patterns.

This fourteen-spot ladybug has nearly rectangular spots on a creamy orange colored body.

This larch ladybug has a distinctive M on its pronotum.

Count the spots on the elytra of this twenty-two-spot ladybug.

The three-striped ladybug looks like a striped candy.

WEIRD AND WONDERFUL

Rosalia Longicorn

This stunning beetle has a beautiful blue exoskeleton and hairy black rings on its antennae.

Giraffe Weevil

Females use their extraordinary necks to build nests, but a male's neck may be up to three times longer.

Violin Beetle

These leaf-like beetles have very flat bodies that let them squeeze into tight spaces in tree bark.

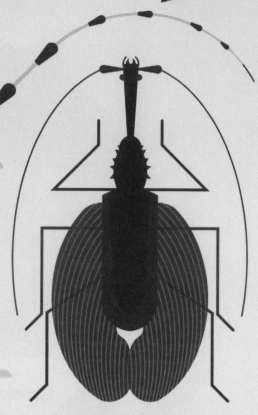

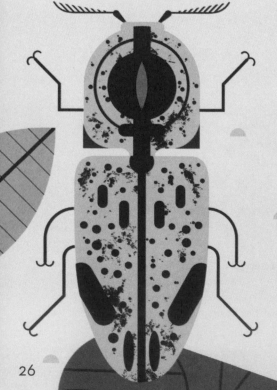

One-Eyed Madagascar Click Beetle

When this beetle finds itself with its legs in the air, it pops its back with a loud clicking noise, bounces upwards, and lands back on its feet.

Frog-Legged Leaf Beetle

It is thought that the males of this species use their powerful back legs as weapons when fighting over females.

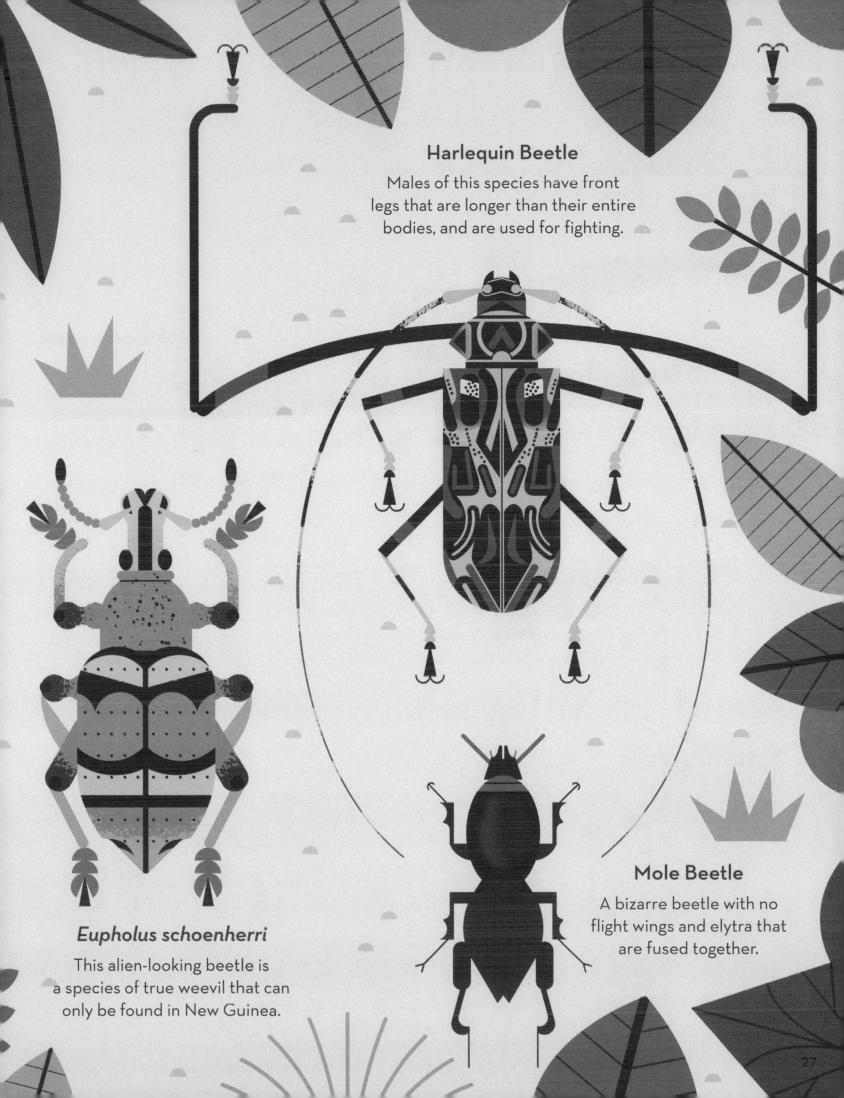

Harlequin Beetle

Males of this species have front legs that are longer than their entire bodies, and are used for fighting.

Eupholus schoenherri

This alien-looking beetle is a species of true weevil that can only be found in New Guinea.

Mole Beetle

A bizarre beetle with no flight wings and elytra that are fused together.

LITTLE AND LARGE

Beetles vary dramatically in size, from the minuscule to the intimidatingly massive, but which is the biggest? The answer to that all depends on what you mean by "big!"

If we're talking about the longest beetle, this title could either belong to the titan beetle or the Hercules beetle. Individuals of both of these colossal critters have been measured at nearly seven inches. That's the size of an adult's hand!

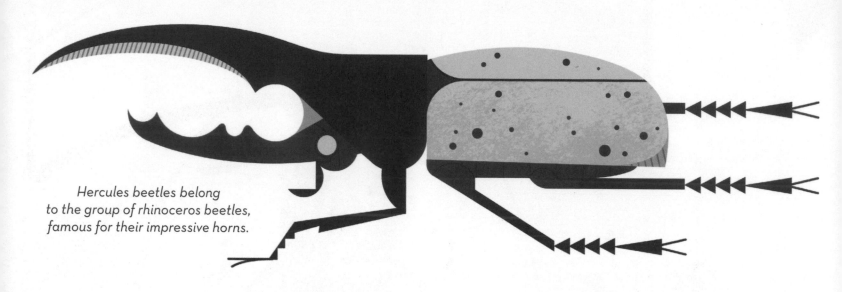

Hercules beetles belong to the group of rhinoceros beetles, famous for their impressive horns.

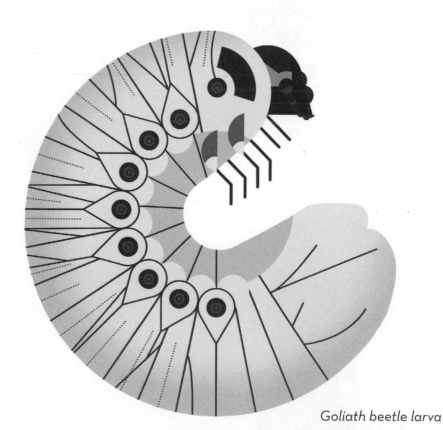

Goliath beetle larva

If you're more interested in the heaviest beetle, you need to see the Goliath beetle. It's an impressive size in adult form, but the true winner is its larva. One gigantic grub can weigh over four ounces, which is about the weight of a banana.

The smallest beetle is thought to be the *Scydosella musawasensis*, a member of the featherwing family. The tiniest individual to be accurately measured came in at a minuscule one hundredth of an inch. That's smaller than the period at the end of this sentence.

---

1 *Onychocerus albitarsis* **2** Horned dung beetle **3** *Eupholus schoenherri*
4 Maquech beetle **5** Seven-spot ladybug **6** Cashew stem girdler **7** Mottled tortoise beetle
8 Harlequin ladybug **9** Titan beetle **10** 22-spot ladybug **11** Rosalia longicorn

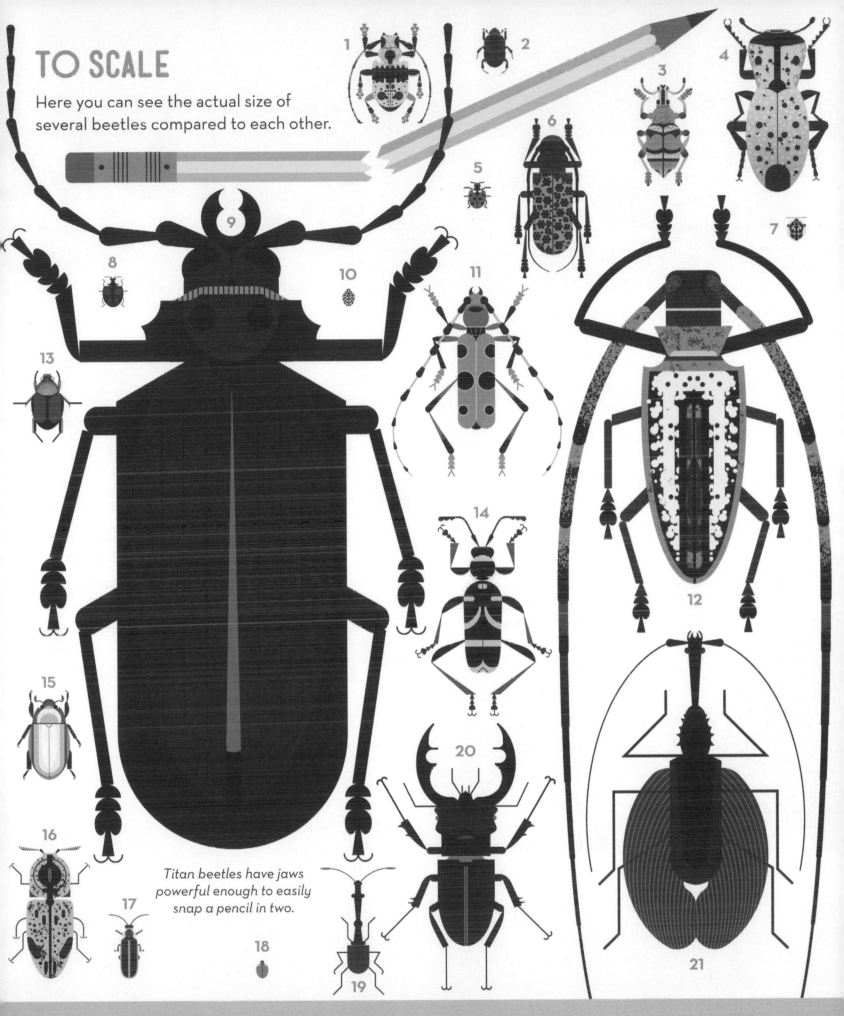

TO SCALE

Here you can see the actual size of several beetles compared to each other.

Titan beetles have jaws powerful enough to easily snap a pencil in two.

12 Wallace's longhorn **13** Japanese beetle **14** *Clytus arietis* **15** *Chrysina aurigans*
16 One-eyed Madagascar click beetle **17** *Photuris pensylvanica*
18 Larch ladybug **19** Giraffe weevil **20** Stag beetle **21** Violin beetle

AND THE AWARD GOES TO...

The award for the strongest beetle goes to the horned dung beetle. This brawny beetle can pull 1,141 times its own body weight. For a human, that would mean the ability to drag an entire airplane filled with vacationers and their luggage. These beetles use their immense strength to drive rivals away from females.

The hotly anticipated award for the best facial hair goes to the aptly-named bearded weevil. The fantastically bushy whiskers of this beetle cover parts of its rostrum, giving it the look of a 19th century English gentleman.

The remarkable red flat bark beetle wins the award for the hardiest beetle. It can withstand incredibly low temperatures that would completely wipe out most other life on Earth. While the adults can tolerate as low as -72° Fahrenheit, it has been proven that the larvae can survive in -148° Fahrenheit by becoming glass-like. They do this by dehydrating themselves and producing a sort of antifreeze within their bodies.

This tiger beetle is the fastest, with a speed of eight feet per second. That may not seem very fast, but if it were the size of a human, it would be moving at the speed of a passenger jet. These beetles move so fast that they go temporarily blind, unable to process enough visual information with their eyes.

The most fashion-minded of all beetles has to be the cashew stem girdler, with its wonderful leopard-print elytra. Females of the species chew a runway for their eggs by gnawing away rings of bark on trees.

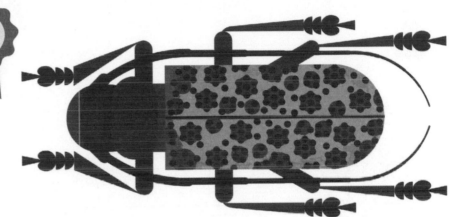

Wallace's longhorn probably nabs the award for the longest antennae. Beetles from the longhorn family typically have very long antennae, but this incredibly large species can have antennae nearly three times the length of its body, reaching more than nine inches.

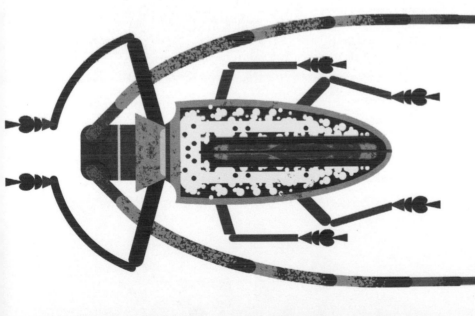

BEETLE MYTHOLOGY

Speak of the Devil

In Irish folklore, the Devil's coach horse beetle was believed to be the Devil in disguise, seeking out sinners and devouring them. People would sometimes conduct rituals in which these unfortunate beetles were burned with fire.

When threatened, the Devil's coach horse beetle raises its abdomen in the air like a scorpion.

A misunderstood deathwatch beetle, trying to find his love.

Bored to Death

Superstition surrounds the deathwatch beetle. They knock their heads in bored wooden burrows to signal to each other, especially at night. People believed this eerie knocking noise was the sound of death coming for them. In truth, the beetles choose mates based on their knocking ability. Many oak timber buildings are infested with these beetles.

Wear Your Heart on Your Chest

In Mayan folklore, a princess was forbidden to marry a prince from a rival clan. They were desperate to be together at any cost, so a compassionate magician turned the prince into a maquech beetle. Now he could live as a brooch on the princess' chest, close to her heart for the rest of his days.

Turning yourself into a beetle definitely shows dedication to the relationship.

On a Roll

Sacred scarabs are seen everywhere in Ancient Egyptian art, jewelry, and hieroglyphs. Khepri was a scarab beetle god that was believed to push the sun across the sky each day, very much like real scarab beetles roll dung.

CONSERVATION

Beetles are amazing creatures that can thrive in all kinds of habitats, but there are several hundreds of species facing serious threat. These beetle populations are dwindling as a direct result of human activity, often because of the destruction of their habitats.

Why should we care? We all know how awesome these beautiful creatures are, but beetles also play a vital role in their ecosystems and help to keep our environment healthy.

An elephant dung beetle rolling its prize.

Dung beetles are responsible for cleaning up the waste of larger animals. Without these beetles, the plains of Africa would be piling up with dung. Yuck!

A hunting vedalia beetle.

Beetles like the vedalia beetle prey on insects that damage agricultural and garden plants, keeping pest populations in check. Without them, many crops would be devastated.

A Phymatodes nitidus and a pinecone.

One species of longhorn is essential to the survival of the giant sequoia trees and coast redwood trees of North America. These beetles feed on the pinecones, causing them to open and allowing the seeds to spread.

How Can We Help?

If you want to help beetles near where you live, you could provide them with a bug hotel. Fill a sturdy wooden box with natural and recycled material to create "rooms" for your insect guests. Ideally, you should put your bug hotel under a tree or next to a hedge around early autumn so that everyone has time to move in before winter arrives. Your beetles will likely be joined by other insects, amphibians, or even mammals in their new accommodation. The more the merrier!

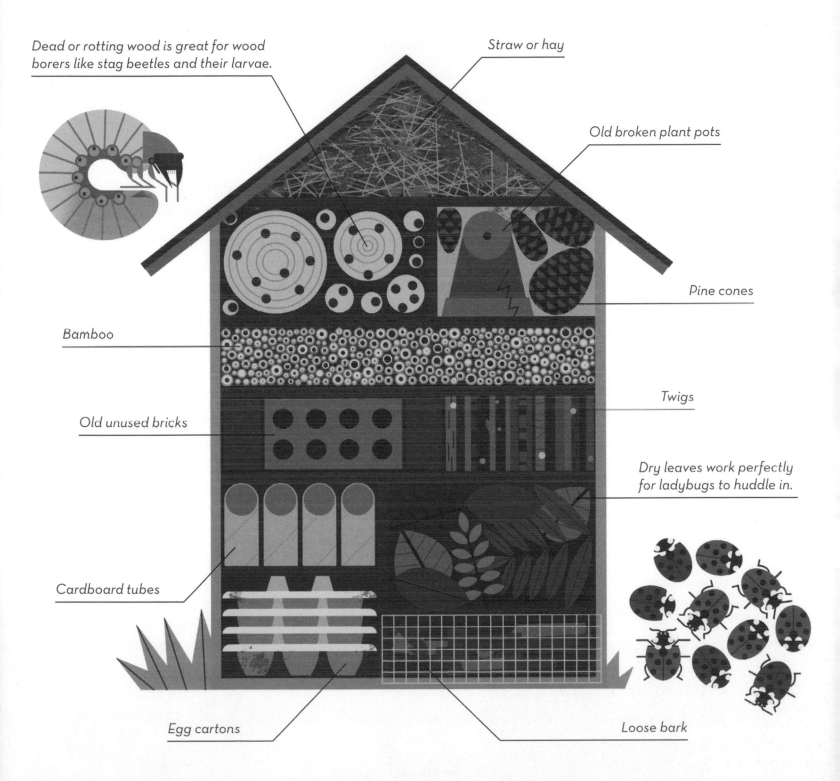

Dead or rotting wood is great for wood borers like stag beetles and their larvae.

Straw or hay

Old broken plant pots

Pine cones

Bamboo

Twigs

Old unused bricks

Dry leaves work perfectly for ladybugs to huddle in.

Cardboard tubes

Egg cartons

Loose bark

Many surveys are conducted across the world to assess how beetle populations are doing. Volunteers are often needed to provide information on sightings of certain species and their location. If you are lucky enough to spot a beetle while you're exploring, maybe you can try to identify it and contact your local researchers.

INDEX

This index covers all the beetles mentioned in this book, but there are thousands more to discover!

ABOUT THE AUTHOR

Owen Davey is an award-winning Illustrator based in Worthing, UK. He has produced more than twenty books published in over twenty-five languages globally and often specializes in non fiction titles for kids. He also works commercially with clients including WWF, Google, National Geographic, and the BBC.

ALSO IN THE SERIES

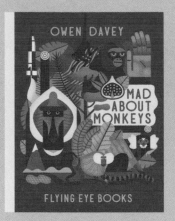

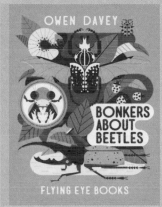

"An absolute wonder . . . with just the right level of information for primary school kids to be truly fascinated and inspired to find out more. Highly recommended."
– *BookTrust*

"An all-round superior non fiction resource."
– *Booklist*

"An arresting and informative guide."
– *Publishers Weekly*

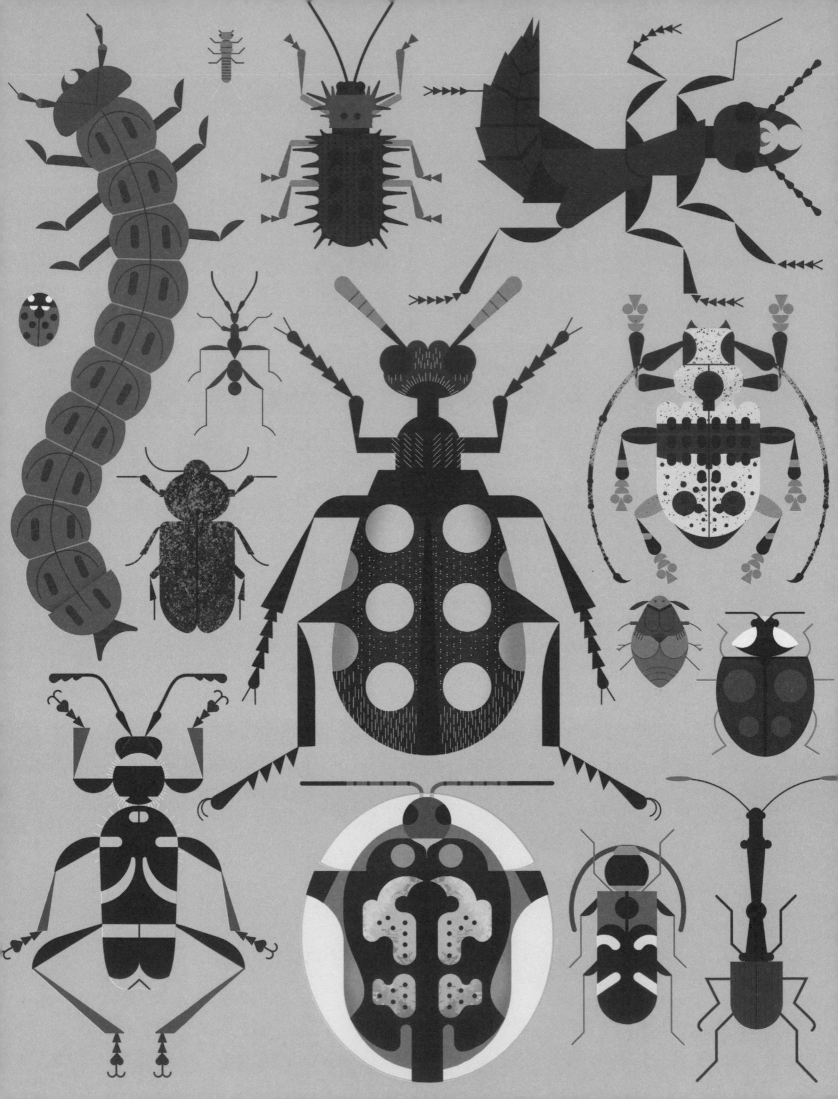